MW00975558

WHAT WE BELIEVE

A PILGRIMAGE
SMALL GROUP GUIDE BY
JEFFREY ARNOLD

NAVPRESS

BRINGING TRUTH TO LIFE
NavPress Publishing Group
P.O. Box 35001, Colorado Springs, Colorado 80935

The Navigators is an international Christian organization. Our mission is to reach, disciple, and equip people to know Christ and to make Him known through successive generations. We envision multitudes of diverse people in the United States and every other nation who have a passionate love for Christ, live a lifestyle of sharing Christ's love, and multiply spiritual laborers among those without Christ.

NavPress is the publishing ministry of The Navigators. NavPress publications help believers learn biblical truth and apply what they learn to their lives and ministries. Our mission is to stimulate spiritual formation among our readers.

© 1997 by Jeff Arnold
All rights reserved. No part of this publication may be reproduced in any form without written permission from NavPress, P.O. Box 35001, Colorado Springs, CO 80935.
ISBN 1-57683-071-3

Cover photo: Danny Lehman/Westlight

Pilgrimage small group study guides are published in conjunction with The Pilgrimage Group, an organization that trains pastors and lay leaders across the United States and Canada in the essentials of small group ministry and leadership. For more information on Pilgrimage training or consulting, call 1-800-477-7787. Or visit the Pilgrimage web site at http//www.pilgrimage.org/training/.

Unless otherwise identified, all Scripture quotations in this publication are taken from the *HOLY BIBLE: NEW INTERNATIONAL VERSION* ® (NIV®). Copyright © 1973, 1978, 1984 by International Bible Society, used by permission of Zondervan Publishing House, all rights reserved. The other version used is *The Message* (MSG) by Eugene H. Peterson, copyright © 1993, 1994, 1995, 1996, used by permission of NavPress Publishing Group.

Printed in the United States of America

1 2 3 4 5 6 7 8 9 10 11 12 13 14 15 / 02 01 00 99 98 97

FOR A FREE CATALOG OF
NAVPRESS BOOKS & BIBLE STUDIES,
CALL 1-800-366-7788 (USA).
IN CANADA, CALL 1-416-499-4615.

Contents

How This Study Guide Works

The Essential Beliefs

When I was young I viewed the Apostles' Creed as a lifeless recitation of biblical facts. What better way to blunt the power of the gospel than to codify its main points and pay them lip service once a week.

Recently, however, I began looking for a framework of core beliefs from which to teach members of my congregation the basic truths of the gospel. What did the New Testament writers hold up as the essentials of faith in Christ? Suddenly it dawned on me: I'm not the first person who ever asked this question.

Within a century or two after Christ's resurrection, His followers were asking the same thing. They had children and new converts to teach, as well as various conflicting schools of thought to sort through. What did those new believers really need to understand? How could they help them discern between truth and error? Years of international consulting and letter writing resulted in a broadly endorsed outline of the faith: the Apostles' Creed.

With newfound appreciation I have come to embrace this historic statement of faith. It has opened up new worlds of reflection and growth. "I believe in God, the Father. . . . I believe in Jesus Christ. . . . I believe in the Holy Spirit. . . ." My heart sings these ideas as God comes alive to me.

Creeds do not have to be dry. We make them dry. They are to be discussed and lived out in the community of faith. The community is where we see the Trinity at work. It is where we practice "the forgiveness of sins." It is where the dry bones of theology receive muscle and sinew, where the breath of the Spirit provides life-giving energy.

The Apostles' Creed is a gift from the church of history to today's church of Jesus Christ. It is is the perfect framework for any exploration of basic Christian beliefs, and forms the outline for this study. Ideal for use by:

- ► small groups
- ► Sunday school classes
- ► new member and inquirer classes
- ► seekers groups

This resource offers seekers and believers an opportunity to partner together in an exciting, relational, hands-on learning approach. During the course of this study, participants will:

- ► discover the essential teachings of the New Testament
- ► engage in individual and group reflection
- ► participate in creative Bible study and group process
- ► work together to solve intriguing theological problems
- ► learn to receive care from other group members
- ► enjoy ongoing support and prayer

What is the Apostles' Creed?

Because of its name, some people believe that the apostles wrote this creed. It is more likely that the Apostles' Creed grew out of the apostles' teaching as the early church tried to systematize Christian thought. At a time when the Scriptures were still not available to the masses, the Apostles' Creed stated core Christian beliefs in a simple manner, easily memorized and transferred from person to person.

The Creed has been a faithful doctrinal foundation for centuries. It has passed the test of scriptural integrity. It has crossed denominational boundaries. It has passed freely through generations and people grou ps. And it has transcended worship styles, as it is used in services ranging from highly liturgical to nonliturgical. Even churches that do not recite it as part of their worship generally subscribe to what it says.

Because of its faithfulness to scriptural teaching and its long history, the Apostles' Creed has a unifying effect for Christians. It may well be that one day in heaven, millions of voices will join together and the "I believe" of the Apostles' Creed will be the "We believe" of eternal worship. Until then, we plant ourselves firmly in the church of Jesus Christ when we embrace this creed as the starting point of theological ("theology" simply means "the study of God") reflection.

Building Community

The life of following Christ was never meant to be solitary. The early Christians pursued it in groups not much larger than the average small group. They met exclusively in homes for the first two hundred years of the movement. By meeting in a small group, you are imitating a time-tested format for spiritual life.

People join small groups for all sorts of reasons: to get to know a few people well, to be cared for, to learn, to grow spiritually. We believe small groups are the ideal settings in which people can learn what it means to take on the character of Christ and practice the process of becoming like Christ. While there are many spiritually helpful things one can do alone or in a large group, a small group offers many advantages. Among other things, group members can:

- ▶ encourage one another in good times and bad
- ▶ ask thoughtful questions when a member has a decision to make
- ▶ listen to God together
- ▶ pray for each other
- ▶ benefit from one another's insights into Scripture
- ▶ acquire a habit of reading the Bible on a regular basis
- ▶ practice loving their neighbors
- ▶ worship God together
- ▶ learn to communicate effectively
- ▶ solve problems together
- ▶ learn to receive care from others
- ▶ experience the pleasure of helping another person grow

This study guide emphasizes reflection and relationship-building. It will help you explore the basics of Christian faith in a nonthreatening group environment. You will engage in reflection, study, interaction, problem solving, prayer, and homework electives so that you can continue learning and growing through the week.

A Modular Approach

Each session is divided into several modules. Suggested times appear at the beginning of each module so that sessions can be completed in 60 to 90 minutes. The modules are:

Overview: The first page of each session briefly describes the objectives for your meeting so that you will know what to expect during the meeting and what results to strive for. You will also learn something about the author's own story as it relates to the topic at hand.

Beginning: Building relationships is a necessary part of any group experience. Each session will have several questions to help you learn who the other members are and where they have been in their lives. The beginning questions also help you begin thinking about a particular issue in preparation for a time of Bible study and problem solving.

The Text: Studying a biblical text is an integral part of this guide. You will examine brief passages from various parts of the Bible. THE MESSAGE by Eugene Peterson and the NEW INTERNATIONAL VERSION have been chosen where appropriate. THE MESSAGE is deliberately relational and will help those familiar with Scripture to see certain passages with new eyes. Since the New Testament was written to be read aloud, you will begin your study by reading the text aloud. Words in bold type are explained in the Reference Notes section.

Understanding the Text: Unless you notice carefully what the text says, you will not be able to interpret it accurately. The questions in this section will help you focus on the key issues and wrestle with what the text means. In this section you will concentrate on the passage in its original first-century context.

Applying the Text: It is not enough simply to understand the passage; you need to apply that understanding to your situation. The questions in this section connect what you have read with how you intend to live.

Assignment: To allow for deeper exploration of the topic at hand, this guide offers homework electives for each session. Make sure that every group member agrees to do work before assigning it.

Prayer: Praying together can be one of the most faith-building and relationship-building activities you do as a group. Suggestions are made to facilitate this time in the group.

Reference Notes: In order to understand the meaning of the text, one needs to know a little about the context in which it was written and the key words and phrases it contains. The Reference Notes module includes background information on characters, cultural practices, word definitions, and so on. You will find entries in this section for those words and phrases in the text printed in bold type.

Food for Thought: This section includes brief commentary on some of the issues raised by the Apostles' Creed.

Additional Resources: A few suggestions for further reading will be offered in relation to the chapter's topic.

Help for the Leader

This guide provides everything the leader needs to facilitate the group's discussion. In each session, the symbol ❶ designates instructions for the leader.

Answers to Common Questions

Who is this material designed for?

- ▶ Anyone who wants to study and discuss basic beliefs that all Christians share.
- ▶ New groups that want to lay a good foundation of relationships as they begin their journey together.

How often should we meet?

- ▶ Once a week is best; every other week also works well.

How long should we meet?

- ▶ You will need at least an hour.
- ▶ Ninety minutes is best—this gives time for more discussion.
- ▶ Some groups may want to meet for two hours, especially if you have more than eight people.

What if we only have 50 minutes?

- ▶ Cut back on the Beginning section and adapt the Applying the Text problem solvers. Read the text quickly and pray only briefly.

Is homework necessary?

- ▶ No, the group can meet with no prior preparation.
- ▶ The assignments will greatly increase what you gain from the group.

SESSION ONE

We Believe

▼ ▼ ▼ ▼ ▼ ▼ ▼ ▼ ▼ ▼ ▼ ▼ ▼ ▼ ▼ ▼ ▼ ▼
Overview   10 minutes

❶ *Make sure that everyone is welcomed to the group and that the room is comfortably arranged. If members do not know each other, exchange names. If they do not know you, introduce yourself to the group, sharing:*

> ▶ *your name*
> ▶ *your role in the group*
> ▶ *several of your goals for the coming weeks*

If others are sharing leadership responsibility with you, perhaps a host/hostess, introduce them as well.

Then, briefly sketch out your agenda for the meeting. What should group members expect to happen? Pass out discussion guides if necessary. Then ask someone to read aloud this story and the objectives that follow.

"I don't believe anything."

I was sitting on the sidewalk after church talking to a young man. A bright, energetic guy, he had experienced more than his share of trials.

"What do you mean?" I asked. "How can you believe nothing?"

"Well, I guess I'm an agnostic. I really don't know what to believe. I think it's neat that you are so convinced about your faith. I'm just not there."

11

Our conversation went on, but as I gazed into the young man's eyes I realized that I was looking into the heart and soul of the Western world. Fed a steady diet of talk shows and pluralistic philosophy, he and others are admittedly unsure of their beliefs.

For every point there is a counterpoint. Experts on either side of every issue barrage us with perspectives and arguments that we would never dream of considering. Spin doctors for politicians and interest groups make wrong seem right and right seem wrong.

Many people are confused. Confused by cultural voices who call them to open-mindedness. Confused by media voices who label belief "narrow-minded." Confused by secular and even Christian institutions of higher learning who dismiss centuries of church and world history as hopelessly dated (wasn't it the medieval church that insisted the world was flat?). Confused by Christians (in the media and world) who claim inside knowledge on everything from politics to what God wants you to do with your life. These are not easy times to discuss what we believe.

We are faced with a number of possible choices. Some of us may choose pluralism, stating our creed that "there is no one absolute truth." Others will select from popular or Christian culture whatever beliefs interest them the most. This guide offers another option: to explore the dimensions of biblical faith as outlined in the Apostles' Creed.

In this session we will:

▶ discuss the importance of beliefs
▶ examine what Scripture says about salvation and belief
▶ explore the Apostles' Creed
▶ discuss issues related to being a small group

▼ ▼ ▼ ▼ ▼ ▼ ▼ ▼ ▼ ▼ ▼ ▼ ▼ ▼ ▼ ▼ ▼ ▼ ▼ ▼
Beginning   15 minutes

❶ *Read aloud this explanation of sharing questions. Once you've read it, go around the room and allow each person to answer the first question before moving to the next one. The leader may choose to answer first each time.*

By sharing our stories with each other, we learn about one another and begin to process how we can affect each others' lives for good. We will earn each others' trust by giving and receiving our stories.

1. What was a unique or funny belief you held earlier in life that you have since discarded? (For example, when I was young I thought that if I crossed my leg too many times, one leg would get shorter than the other!)

2. Which phrase best describes the importance of religion to your childhood household?

   ❏ strongly held beliefs
   ❏ no attention given to religion
   ❏ anything religious is fine
   ❏ fervent love of God freely passed on
   ❏ other:

The word *belief* is easily dismissed in modern usage as little more than a passing thought ("I believe it is going to rain today"). But in Scripture, belief carries the same meaning as words like faith, allegiance, and ultimate trust.

3. When you were a teenager, what was a belief or allegiance you had that strongly influenced what you did with your time and money?

   ❏ I was devoted to a particular musical style.
   ❏ I thought science or reason could solve all of the world's problems.
   ❏ I believed in having fun.
   ❏ My boyfriend/girlfriend was the most important thing in life.
   ❏ I believed in world peace, environmental issues, etc.
   ❏ other:

▼ ▼ ▼ ▼ ▼ ▼ ▼ ▼ ▼ ▼ ▼ ▼ ▼ ▼ ▼ ▼ ▼ ▼ ▼ ▼
The Text   5 minutes

Those who expect Scripture to be a systematic book of doctrine are disappointed. Scripture uses many genres to communicate truth, including poetry, letters, and narrative. However, a text-book format is nowhere found. Moved by the Spirit, biblical authors used images and stories (among other means) to carry God's truth to His followers. This type of communication reveals God as less concerned with systematic theology than He is with interacting with the hearts and minds of His people.

Nonetheless, Scripture's nonsystematic structure does not belie an absence of God's truth. On the contrary, Scripture purports to reveal the truth, Jesus claims to *be* the truth, and the Holy Spirit's stated role is to teach us the truth. In Romans 10:5-13, the apostle Paul discusses the foundations of a Christian's belief structure by linking truth to our faith.

❶ *Have someone read the text aloud. You may also read some or all of the reference notes on page 19.*

The earlier revelation was intended simply to get us ready for the Messiah, who then puts everything right for those who trust him to do it. Moses wrote that anyone who insists on using the law code to live right before God soon discovers it's not so easy—every detail of life regulated by fine print! But trusting God to shape the right living in us is a different story—**no precarious climb up to heaven to recruit the Messiah, no dangerous descent into hell to rescue the Messiah.** So what exactly was Moses saying?

> "The word that saves is right here,
>   as near as the tongue in your mouth,
>   as close as the heart in your chest."

It's the word of faith that welcomes God to go to work and set things right for us. This is the core of our preaching. Say the welcoming word to God—"Jesus is my master"—embracing, body and soul, God's work of doing in us what he did in raising Jesus from the dead. That's it. You're not "doing" anything; you're simply calling out to God, trusting him to do it for you. That's salvation. With your whole being you embrace God setting things right, and then you **say it, right out loud:** "God has set everything right between him and me!"

Scripture reassures us, "No one who trusts God like this— **heart and soul**—will ever regret it." It's exactly the same no matter what a person's religious background may be: the same God for all of us, acting the same incredibly generous way to everyone who calls out for help. "Everyone who calls, 'Help, God!' gets help."

(Romans 10:5-13, MSG)

14

Understanding the Text 10 minutes

4. According to Paul, what are the problems associated with attempting to live by the "law code"?

5. What actions allow us to be made right with God?

We noted earlier that belief is the same as faith, allegiance, and complete trust. It is not an apathetic acceptance of doctrinal code, but an active willingness to embrace God and God's ways. The text says this kind of belief:

▶ trusts God (completely)
▶ calls out to God
▶ welcomes God
▶ embraces God's work, body and soul
▶ says out loud, "God has set everything right between Himself and me!"

6. Whom do you know whose belief in God reflects these realities? How do they show this kind of faith?

7. As a group (and based on this passage), attempt to summarize what this passage says about:
   ❐ why belief is important
   ❐ how we come to believe in God
   ❐ what happens to us when we believe in God

8. This passage assumes that Scripture is important ("through God's revealed Word") to our beliefs. How does Scripture help shape a Christian's beliefs?

▼ ▼ ▼ ▼ ▼ ▼ ▼ ▼ ▼ ▼ ▼ ▼ ▼ ▼ ▼ ▼ ▼ ▼
Applying the Text   20 minutes

9. What might this passage's focus on life-changing belief communicate to the following stereotypical persons?

❏ The fundamentalist who verbally beats up anyone who believes differently than he does
❏ The agnostic who thinks everybody is going to heaven
❏ The New Ager who thinks God is everything, and everything is God
❏ The theologian who reduces everything to definable categories
❏ The pluralist who doesn't care what you believe as long as you believe

Throughout history the church has used several means to delineate foundational beliefs. A *creed* is a statement of belief (*credo* is Latin for "I believe") encompassing the essentials of the Christian faith. A *confession* is a statement of core beliefs particular to a denomination or branch of the church (for example, the Westminster Confession of Faith is a "Reformed" standard). A *catechism* is the teaching tool used to establish church members in the particulars of their confession (the Larger Catechism accompanies the Westminster Confession).

Page 6 gives some background on the Apostles' Creed. It is a remarkably resilient statement of belief because many Christians recognize that it contains the foundation of our life together in Christ.

What follows is a modern English translation of the Creed. (Versions vary slightly. For instance, some say "Holy Ghost" instead of "Holy Spirit." Some use "holy catholic" rather than "holy Christian." "Catholic" in this context is an old English word meaning "universal.")

I believe in God, the Father Almighty,
    creator of heaven and earth.
I believe in Jesus Christ, His only Son, our Lord,
    who was conceived by the Holy Spirit,
    born of the Virgin Mary,
    suffered under Pontius Pilate,
    was crucified, died, and was buried.
    He descended to the dead,
    On the third day He rose again.
    He ascended into heaven,
    and is seated at the right hand of the Father.
    He will come again to judge the living and the dead.
I believe in the Holy Spirit,
    the holy Christian church,
    the communion of saints,
    the forgiveness of sins,
    the resurrection of the body,
    and the life everlasting. Amen.

10. What aspects of the Creed are most attractive to you?

11. What questions does the Creed raise for you?

❶ *You may want to refer back to the issues raised in question 11 to supplement your discussions in future sessions.*

Assignment   5 minutes

Belief is foundational to life. Therefore, religious thought permeates everything we do. Assign one of the following to each group member (only if every member agrees to participate):

    ▶ Watch a television show and try to discern the show's underlying assumptions, values, and perception of "salvation."

- Do the same thing for a movie instead of television.

- Interview a person to find out his or her beliefs regarding truth and salvation. Do not comment, just listen.

- Walk through a mall or public place and locate as many religious symbols as possible. (If you look carefully, you'll see beyond the obvious cross necklace or Grateful Dead T-shirts.)

- Keep a journal with you throughout the week and write down everything you do that is based on a belief. For example, when you flip on a light switch, you expect light.

Prayer ▼ ▼ ▼ ▼ ▼ ▼ ▼ ▼ ▼ ▼ ▼ ▼ ▼ ▼ ▼ ▼ ▼ ▼ ▼ 10 minutes

Before you pray together, discuss the following ground rules for being in this group. Add to the list as you see fit, and then make a covenant of trust with one another. We promise to practice:

- Acceptance—To affirm one anothers' contributions
- Confidentiality—That what is spoken in this group will remain in the group
- Openness—That we will be honest and forthright with one another
- Self-discipline—That if the group agrees to do homework, we will come prepared
- Courtesy—That we will come on time
- Listening—That we will not monopolize time so that others can speak
- Other:

Once you have agreed on your group ground rules, stand in a circle and recite the Creed aloud as a prayer of faith to God. (Those who have questions or objections to the Creed may choose to remain silent. That's fine.)

Reference Notes

Setting: Paul wrote the book of Romans to people he had not had an opportunity to pastor. His intent was to offer a basics-of-the-faith letter in place of his personal ministry. This particular passage occurs in the context of Paul's concern for the salvation of Israel (from Romans 9-11). Hence, his reference to "the law code" refers to the system of rituals by which Jews expressed their relationship with God. Paul contrasts the Jewish view of the centrality of religious ritual with his own view that faith in Christ, openly declared, is the central expression of relationship with God.

The earlier revelation: The Old Testament.

No precarious climb up to heaven to recruit the Messiah, no dangerous descent into hell to rescue the Messiah: Here Paul makes a tongue-in-cheek comment about those who would do anything to save themselves, except to believe.

Say it, right out loud: Belief means nothing until it manifests itself in our conversation—because our words reveal who we are and what we believe. That is why stating our conviction is as important as believing it.

Heart and soul: In this passage are references to every area of our being: our motives, our thoughts, our minds, our words, our deeds, our hopes, and our dreams. God's truth must permeate each area.

Food for Thought

"I believe."

► *Is there absolute truth?* Yes. The statement that there is no absolute truth is in fact a statement of an absolute truth. Somewhere out there, something or someone is right about ultimate reality. Jesus proclaimed absolute truth when He said in John 14:6, "I am the way and the truth and the life. No one comes to the Father except through

19

me." In John 14:17, Jesus called the Spirit, "the Spirit of truth." Ultimately, each attempt at framing truth (including atheism, evolution, and Christianity) requires a leap of faith.

► *Can I believe firmly in truth yet still be open to new information?* Many thoughtful people fear becoming narrow-minded when they consider embracing truth. But nobody can have everything 100% figured out. Theological reflection demands a single-minded, passionate pursuit of God, mingled with the humility that our understanding is limited and broken. Thus, our interaction with the world is not as those who "have arrived," but as pilgrim seekers who openly and freely engage our world in conversation with the Spirit who lives in us.

▼ ▼ ▼ ▼ ▼ ▼ ▼ ▼ ▼ ▼ ▼ ▼ ▼ ▼ ▼ ▼ ▼ ▼ ▼
Additional Resources

1. Briscoe, Stuart. *The Apostles' Creed*. Wheaton, Ill.: Harold Shaw, 1994.

2. Dunnam, Maxie. *This Is Christianity*. Nashville, Tenn: Abingdon, 1994.

3. Little, Paul. *Know Why You Believe*. Downers Grove, Ill.: InterVarsity, 1973.

4. Wells, David F. *No Place for Truth*. Grand Rapids, Mich.: Eerdmans, 1993.

We Believe in God the Father

Overview   10 minutes

❶ *Make sure that any newcomers are introduced and given the appropriate materials. Exchange names if memories need to be refreshed.*

Allow several people to share what they learned from their homework (if the group did not do homework, ask several people to recap what they learned from the last session). Then ask someone to read aloud this story and the objectives that follow.

When I was a teenager, my father and I raised bees. Almost every Saturday from spring through fall, Dad and I would drive to the farm where the bees were kept.

We invariably interrupted the bees in the course of their busy lives. Using a smoke gun, we would take the top off each hive and perform a series of maintenance procedures. In doing so, we became witnesses of the various activities of a hive.

Street cleaner bees struggled with broken pieces of comb. Drones (the males) did as little as possible. The queen faithfully laid thousands of eggs in the comb. The comb was raised and prepared by builder bees. Worker bees brought nectar and pollen to the hive, and cafeteria bees worked the nectar into honey and the pollen into sustenance for the young bees being hatched.

A beehive is a wonderful sight to behold. Yet, as structured and disciplined as bees are, they also have some self-defeating tendencies. They tend to build honeycomb everywhere, creating dead-end passsageways and blocking off portions of the hive. They often hatch too many queen bee eggs, creating "palace coups" and internal squabbles that destroy a hive's efficiency. And sometimes they will leave a hive full of honey and just move to another location.

As beekeepers we had to go to the hive and, through routine maintenance, keep things going as smoothly as possible. We were not able to solve all of the bees' problems, but our intervention kept them healthier and happier.

Our efforts were not much appreciated. The bees would get worked into a frenzy over our presence and would want us out. Sometimes my father and I got angry bees in our clothes. The results, as you may imagine, were not pleasant!

Our experience with the bees helps me reflect on how we humans relate to God. Like the bees, we create systems, governments, and societies that allow us to function as we feel most comfortable. Unfortunately, we possess some self-defeating tendencies. According to Scripture, God becomes involved in our world, redeeming and saving us from ourselves. Of course, we are not often happy with His presence, and we attempt to control, remove, or even destroy Him.

When we say in the Creed, "I believe in God, the Father Almighty," we are admitting that there is an all-powerful Presence in the universe. We are also admitting our need for His intervention.

The Apostles' Creed is "Trinitarian" in structure: that is, it recognizes one God in three Persons. The first Person, the Father, we discuss in this session. The second Person, the Son, we discuss in the succeeding three sessions. The third Person, the Spirit, we discuss in session 6. In this session we will:

> ▶ discuss different perceptions of God's involvement in the universe
> ▶ examine the nature and character of God the "Father"
> ▶ consider the life implications of an all-powerful God

▼ ▼ ▼ ▼ ▼ ▼ ▼ ▼ ▼ ▼ ▼ ▼ ▼ ▼ ▼ ▼ ▼ ▼ ▼
Beginning   15 minutes

❶ *Go around the room and allow each person to answer the first question before moving to the next one. The leader should answer first each time.*

1. What is a recollection (question, thought, experience) about God you have retained from your childhood?

2. When you were young, which of the following images most closely resembled your perception of God?

   ❏ Santa Claus—jovial, overweight, always giving
   ❏ Lone Ranger—mysterious, unknown, aloof
   ❏ Terminator—waiting for you to "blow it" so that He can destroy you
   ❏ Absentee landlord—not paying much attention, allows bad things to happen, doesn't seem to care
   ❏ Judge—keeping track of all your wrongs

▼ ▼ ▼ ▼ ▼ ▼ ▼ ▼ ▼ ▼ ▼ ▼ ▼ ▼ ▼ ▼ ▼ ▼ ▼ ▼
The Text   5 minutes

Jesus used the word "Father" seventeen times in the Sermon on the Mount (Matthew 5–7) to refer to God, and over forty times in the Gospel of Matthew (John's Gospel has even more). It is the name Jesus used most often to refer to the first Person of the Trinity. Not only did Jesus refer to God as His Father, but He also offered the Father to us (as "our Father").

❶ *Have someone read the text aloud. You may also read some or all of the reference notes on page 28.*

"You have heard that it was said, 'Love your neighbor and hate your enemy.' But I tell you: Love your enemies and pray for those who persecute you, that you may be sons of your Father in heaven. He causes his sun to rise on the evil and the good, and sends rain on the righteous and the unrighteous. . . . Be perfect, therefore, as your heavenly Father is perfect.

"Be careful not to do your 'acts of righteousness' before men, to be seen by them. If you do, you will have no reward from your Father in heaven. . . . But when you give to the needy, do not let your left hand know what your right hand is doing, so that your giving may be in secret. Then your Father, who sees what is done in secret, will reward you.

"But when you pray, do not be like the hypocrites, for they love to pray standing in the synagogues and on the street corners to be seen by men. . . . When you pray, go into your room, close the door and pray to your Father, who is unseen. Then your Father, who sees what is done in secret, will reward you. . . . your Father knows what you need before you ask him.

"This, then, is how you should pray:

"'Our Father in heaven,
hallowed be your name,
your kingdom come,
your will be done
 on earth as it is in heaven.
Give us today our daily bread.
Forgive us our **debts**,
 as we also have forgiven our debtors.
And lead us not into temptation,
but deliver us from the evil one.'

For if you forgive men when they sin against you, your heavenly Father will also forgive you. But if you do not forgive men their sins, your Father will not forgive your sins."

(Matthew 5:43-45,48; 6:1,3-6,8-15)

▼ ▼ ▼ ▼ ▼ ▼ ▼ ▼ ▼ ▼ ▼ ▼ ▼ ▼ ▼ ▼ ▼ ▼ ▼ ▼
Understanding the Text   10 minutes

3. Each of the four paragraphs in this text contains a separate, but interrelated, teaching. What is Jesus telling His disciples about:

   a. relating to our enemies?

   b. helping the poor?

   c. praying?

   d. forgiving those who wrong us?

4. In all of these statements, Jesus is trying to teach His disciples about God.

   a. Why do you think Jesus uses the word "Father" so extensively?

   b. What negative feelings might the term "Father" bring up for some hearers?

   c. What positive meaning does Jesus intend for the word "Father" to convey?

   d. Why do you suppose Jesus repeatedly calls Him "your" Father?

5. Let each member of your group select one of the following references from the text and explain what it reveals about who God is and what God does?

   ❐ "He causes his sun to rise on the evil and the good"
   ❐ "your heavenly Father is perfect"
   ❐ "your Father will [or will not] reward you"
   ❐ "your Father, who sees what is done in secret"
   ❐ "and pray to your Father, who is unseen"
   ❐ "your Father knows what you need before you ask"
   ❐ "Our Father in heaven, hallowed be your name"
   ❐ "your heavenly Father will also forgive you"
   ❐ "your Father will not forgive your sins"

6. Based on the passage you have just studied, try to construct an expanded statement of faith (at least four or five sentences) that addresses what you believe about the first Person of the Trinity.

   ❐ Who is God?
   ❐ What do we know about God the Father?
   ❐ How does God act toward us?

Applying the Text

7. Jesus teaches us many things about the Father in this passage, referring to Him as all-knowing, all-powerful, loving, forgiving, providing, and caring. What behaviors or attitudes might we be motivated to adopt based on these characteristics?

8. We are first called to believe in "God, the Father Almighty." We are then asked to respond to His presence and work in our lives. How might you encourage the following people, based on what the text has said about God the Father?

   a. Nathan is a chronically unhappy person. His job is never right. His family is more a nuisance than anything else. His lifestyle is always too cramped. His church always does the wrong things. Whenever he gets close to a person, he invariably does something to offend that person and drive him or her away—including his family. One day as you are talking to him, the past comes up. Nathan confides that his father never accepted him. He also has never felt close to God. How might God the Father be able to help him?

   b. Shelly has spent her whole life trying to get close to her family, especially to her father. Her relationships with males reflect her desire to have a deep relationship with a man—but almost every man ends up using her. A few years ago she gave her life to Jesus and prayed that God would make a difference in her family relationships. Unfortunately, her father does not seem to respond, and he still finds ways to put her down and even use her. She confides with tears that she is devastated and unsure about what to believe or do. How might God the Father be able to help her?

Assignment   5 minutes

Some or all of your group members may interview friends, relatives, or work associates about their beliefs in God. You may ask them the following questions, or create your own:

▶ Who or what is your ultimate reality or God?

▶ What are the characteristics and activities of your ultimate reality or God?

▶ How do you learn about your ultimate reality or God? (From a set of writings? From experience? From yourself? From other people?)

Prayer   5 minutes

Discuss the following prayer ground rules. Add to the list or adapt it according to your situation.

▶ *Be conversational.* The group is not a place for impressive theological prayers. Many people need to feel comfortable praying for the first time out loud—so keep prayer relaxed and relational.

▶ *Be brief.* The first people who pray in a group setting are usually comfortable praying in public. They can end up covering all requests in a lengthy prayer. A good practice is to hold the first two "pray-ers" to two sentences each.

▶ *Be courteous.* There are several ways to practice courtesy in prayer. First, keep requests personal and limited to intimate family and friends. This is not the time to address distant relatives or international events, which are best left to organized prayer meetings. Second, be as brief as possible when sharing requests so that everyone will have time to share.

▶ *Be sensitive.* A small group is not the place to attempt to counsel another person.

▶ *Be real.* Most of the prayer times in this resource encourage you to respond to the issue being studied. If your group committed to confidentiality—see page 18—you can be honest about what you need God to do in your life.

Stand in a circle. Allow each person to respond to the statement, "One reason God, the Father Almighty, is important to me is. . . ." Hold hands if you are comfortable doing so. Let each person pray aloud, beginning with the leader. Consider praying by name for the individuals in your group, asking God to help each of you experience God in a deeper way. If you would rather pray silently, please say "Amen" aloud to let the other people know you are finished.

▼ ▼ ▼ ▼ ▼ ▼ ▼ ▼ ▼ ▼ ▼ ▼ ▼ ▼ ▼ ▼ ▼ ▼ ▼
Reference Notes

Setting: The larger context of this teaching is the Sermon on the Mount, and the immediate context is best summarized by Matthew 6:1: "Be careful not to do your 'acts of righteousness' before men, to be seen by them." Jesus is concerned that His followers live out their faith in a "pure" form. In this case, purity has less to do with some intangible inner quality of believers, and more to do with our interactions with the Father. Two themes running through this section of the Sermon on the Mount are the character qualities necessary to live out our faith and the interaction with God necessary to cause our character to develop.

debts: A Jewish word for "sin."

and lead us not into temptation: This phrase is difficult to explain. The word "temptation" might mean "trials," or the phrasing of the request might imply that we are crying from our soul for God to sanctify us by His power. In this latter perspective, sanctification (God's purifying work in our lives) is a positive statement of the prayer (lead us out of temptation).

▼ ▼ ▼ ▼ ▼ ▼ ▼ ▼ ▼ ▼ ▼ ▼ ▼ ▼ ▼ ▼ ▼ ▼ ▼

Food for Thought

"I believe in God, the Father Almighty."

▶ *What are we to make of attempts to create a gender-transcendent God?* Study of Scripture leads to an understanding that God, who goes by numerous descriptive names in the Bible, defies true definition and understanding. Gender does not adequately describe Him. Therefore, He is not a "guy." However, Scripture uses the masculine pronoun to refer to God and (usually) masculine images to describe Him. In addition, Jesus called God "Father" repeatedly. Attempts to dismiss scriptural authors (and Jesus) as sexist do not adequately take into account the heart of God, which is carefully revealed in many of the gender-specific descriptions of Him. What many have found is that relating to a gender-neutral God often yields the unintended consequence of lost intimacy with Him.

▶ *How do we reconcile the (apparent) Old Testament God of judgment with the (apparent) New Testament God of grace?* My perspective is that justice, grace, and wrath are themes not just of one testament, but of both. The difference between the testaments is that Jesus is promised in the Old and revealed in the New. Thus, God's expression of sovereign grace is more concentrated in the New Testament. But the Old Testament is also full of God's mercy, grace, favor, and patience. Even the prophets, noted for their strong language, often spoke of God's grace (see Psalm 103 and Jeremiah 30 as examples).

▶ *Is God an all-powerful sovereign, or a well-meaning guide?* Questions related to sovereignty, predestination, and free will have engaged Christians for centuries, especially since the Reformation (1400s). Some traditions place a higher premium on God's power; others on His willingness to let us choose. One brief comment: God's sovereignty and human free will are both taught in Scripture. God must have some unimaginable way of working out the apparent contradictions.

Additional Resources ▼▼▼▼▼▼▼▼▼▼▼▼▼▼▼▼▼▼▼▼

1. Packer, J. I. *Knowing God.* Downers Grove, Ill.: InterVarsity, 1973.

2. Pinnock, Clark and Robert Brow. *Unbounded Love: A Good News Theology for the 21st Century.* Downers Grove, Ill.: InterVarsity, 1994.

3. Sproul, R. C. *Pleasing God.* Wheaton, Ill.: Tyndale, 1988.

We Believe in Jesus Christ: Our Lord

▼ ▼ ▼ ▼ ▼ ▼ ▼ ▼ ▼ ▼ ▼ ▼ ▼ ▼ ▼ ▼ ▼ ▼ ▼
Overview   10 minutes

❶ *Allow several people to share what they learned from their homework (if the group did not do homework, ask several people to recap what they learned from the last session). Then ask someone to read aloud this overview and the objectives that follow.*

Have you ever anticipated something with great excitement, only to discover that the real event was nowhere near as grand as the build-up in your mind?

Aside from marriage and parenthood—which provide my life with pleasures and challenges that rival any expectations I might have had—I have discovered time and again that my dreams exceed reality. I recall, for example, the publication of my first book (*The Big Book on Small Groups*, InterVarsity). For two years of the editing and typesetting process I had to stifle my excitement. When I was told that my book would be arriving in the mail "any day," I almost lost it. Each day I would drive home and check the mail, almost bursting with anticipation.

One day my wife called, and the package had arrived. For several days I felt really special. We mailed copies to our families, and I displayed one proudly on my desk. But then the luster wore off, and life went on. Now, when I use my books in ministry, I have to purchase them just as everyone else does.

We experience such dynamics frequently. The new car that had all of the gadgets becomes old and is eventually traded for

31

another. The job that was going to change our lives somehow fizzles. The greatest vacation we could ever plan becomes a Chevy Chase nightmare. The toy or tool or recognition that was supposed to fulfill us doesn't last long enough for us to enjoy it.

You cannot embrace material things, circumstances, or even awards. Once they have been lived, polished, and shelved, a fundamental emptiness remains.

I can think of no greater reason to seek a Messiah. Tired of life's mirages, seekers want something (someone?) lasting to embrace and hold. For each seeker, the Creed cries out, "I believe . . . in Jesus Christ, His only Son, our Lord." Jesus saves us from our mundane existence. He redeems our lives from self-destructive behaviors. He beckons us into the very throne room of the Father. He calls us to live for a higher reason and according to a higher standard.

He who cannot be seen offers blessings that are tangible and life-changing. How ironic that material rewards which can be seen often promise more than they can deliver, like a rainbow you can see but not touch.

In this session we will:

▶ discuss our life needs and goals
▶ examine what Scripture says about Jesus the Messiah
▶ ponder the difference Jesus the Messiah makes in our lives

▼ ▼ ▼ ▼ ▼ ▼ ▼ ▼ ▼ ▼ ▼ ▼ ▼ ▼ ▼ ▼ ▼ ▼ ▼
Beginning   15 minutes

❶ *Go around the room and allow each person to answer the first question before moving on to the next one. The leader should answer first each time.*

1. What is something you really wanted in life and had to wait (perhaps a long time) for?

2. What is something you eagerly anticipated, then experienced disappointment over when it arrived?

3. Examine the list of desires below. Which three would have been on top of your list as a teenager? How about now?

❏ millions of dollars
❏ a large dream house and several vacation homes
❏ guaranteed good health for me and my family
❏ a challenging life
❏ very good looks
❏ a loving spouse
❏ popularity, friendship, and approval
❏ a chance to make a difference in the world
❏ a wonderful personality
❏ peace and joy
❏ the ability to tell others about Jesus naturally and effectively
❏ a happy home
❏ the perfect job (what would that job be?)
❏ other:

4. If your desires or priorities have changed over the years, what has accounted for that change?

5. What do you suppose your desires will look like twenty years from now?

▼ ▼ ▼ ▼ ▼ ▼ ▼ ▼ ▼ ▼ ▼ ▼ ▼ ▼ ▼ ▼ ▼ ▼
The Text   5 minutes

Here the apostle Peter encourages believers to grow in their faith by interacting with Jesus, the Messiah.

❶ *Have someone read the text aloud. You may also read some or all of the reference notes on page 38.*

I, Simon Peter, am a servant and apostle of Jesus **Christ**. I write this to you whose experience with God is as life-changing as ours, all due to our God's straight dealing and the intervention of our God and Savior, Jesus Christ. Grace and peace to you many times over as you deepen in your experience with God and Jesus, our Master.

Everything that goes into a life of pleasing God has been miraculously given to us by getting to know, personally and intimately, the One who invited us to God. The best invitation we ever received! We were also given absolutely terrific promises to pass on to you—your tickets to participation in the life of God after you turned your back on a world corrupted by lust.

So don't lose a minute in building on what you've been given, complementing your basic faith with good character, spiritual understanding, alert discipline, passionate patience, reverent wonder, warm friendliness, and generous love, each dimension fitting into and developing the others. With these qualities active and growing in your lives, no grass will grow under your feet, no day will pass without its reward as you mature in your experience of our Master Jesus. Without these qualities you can't see what's right before you, oblivious that your old sinful life has been wiped off the books.

So, friends, confirm God's invitation to you, his choice of you. Don't put it off; do it now. Do this, and you'll have your life on a firm footing, the streets paved and the way wide open into the eternal kingdom of our Master and Savior, Jesus Christ. . . .

We weren't, you know, just wishing on a star when we laid the facts out before you regarding the powerful return of our Master, Jesus Christ. We were there for the **preview**! We saw it with our own eyes: Jesus resplendent with light from God the Father as the voice of Majestic Glory spoke: "This is my Son, marked by my love, focus of all my delight."

(2 Peter 1:1-11,16-17, MSG)

▼ ▼ ▼ ▼ ▼ ▼ ▼ ▼ ▼ ▼ ▼ ▼ ▼ ▼ ▼ ▼ ▼ ▼ ▼
Understanding the Text   10 minutes

6. Have someone read these names (taken from this text), and the brief descriptions that follow:

   ☐ Jesus—which means, "Jehovah (God) Saves."
   ☐ Christ—which means, the "Anointed One" (see reference note)

❏ God—the Ultimate Reality, possessing all of God's attributes
❏ Savior—the One who saves us from the world, from ourselves, from evil
❏ Master—our Lord, the One we follow and serve with our whole being
❏ Son (of God)—in intimate family relationship with God

In a sentence or two, summarize what you learn about Jesus from these names.

7. In the first paragraph Peter says, "I write this to you whose experience with God is as life-changing as ours, all due to our God's straight dealing and the intervention of our God and Savior, Jesus Christ."

    a. What are some biblical or other examples you are aware of that reveal God's "straight dealings" with humans?

    b. What are some biblical or other examples you are aware of that reveal how Jesus has intervened in human affairs?

8. Peter assumes in the second paragraph that our key to a deeper relationship with God is in getting to know Jesus. How can modern persons get to know Jesus better?

9. We are told to build on our "basic faith" with some additional characteristics of maturity. Discuss what each of
these might look like in real life:

❑ good character
❑ spiritual understanding
❑ alert discipline
❑ passionate patience
❑ reverent wonder
❑ warm friendliness
❑ generous love

10. How might Jesus, the Master, help us to implement those
experiences?

Applying the Text 20 minutes

11. Looking back over this passage for what you have learned
about Jesus and His Lordship over our lives, create a statement of faith that addresses the following:

❑ Who is Jesus?
❑ What does Jesus do?
❑ What does it mean that Jesus is "Master"?

12. Allow anyone to respond to this statement as he or she
feels led: "This is what Jesus means to me. . . ."

❶ *Give everyone a chance to respond to question 13.*

13. Complete this sentence: "Of the maturity traits listed in
question 9,

❑ one that Jesus has helped me with is . . .
❑ one that I need Jesus to help me with is . . .

Assignment
5 minutes

Find at least one advertisement that promises something it most likely will not deliver. You can clip newspaper or magazine ads, or jot down information from a billboard or television commercial. You may journal, reflect, and ultimately discuss how our culture continuously makes promises it cannot keep (as opposed to Jesus, who keeps all His promises).

Prayer
5 minutes

Look over the following ground rules (discussed in your last session) to remind yourselves about the fundamentals of group prayer.

- ► *Be conversational.*
- ► *Be brief.*
- ► *Be courteous.*
- ► *Be sensitive.*
- ► *Be real.*

Stand in a circle. Hold hands if you are comfortable doing so. Let each person pray aloud, beginning with the leader. Consider praying by name for the members in your group, asking Jesus to accomplish in your lives the kinds of issues discussed in question 13. If you would rather pray silently, please say "Amen" aloud to let the other people know you are finished.

Reference Notes

Setting: In 2 Peter, the apostle is writing a second letter (to complement 1 Peter) to Christians scattered throughout the Roman empire and who were being persecuted for their beliefs.

Christ: It was a Hebrew custom to pour oil on a person's head when setting him apart for special service. Kings and prophets in particular were anointed with oil. After both the northern and southern kingdoms of Israel were destroyed, the Jews lived under foreign rulers and had no king of their own. The prophets foretold that a king of the ancient royal bloodline would eventually be born and would rule again. This king was referred to as *ha mashiach*, which means "the Anointed One." *Mashiach* has come into English as "Messiah," and its Greek translation, *Christos*, as "Christ."

So don't lose a minute in building on what you've been given: The traits listed here are actually disciplines that Peter expects believers to practice so that their relationship with God will deepen. The active practice of these traits can occur only within the framework of a life-changing relationship with Christ. Trying to have God's "good character," for example, without Jesus is like attempting to play professional baseball without a fielder's glove.

preview: A reference to the time when Peter and two other disciples saw Jesus transfigured with divine light (Matthew 17:1-8).

▼ ▼ ▼ ▼ ▼ ▼ ▼ ▼ ▼ ▼ ▼ ▼ ▼ ▼ ▼ ▼ ▼ ▼ ▼
Food for Thought

"I believe in Jesus Christ, His only Son, our Lord."

▶ *Was/is Jesus God?* In John 8:58 He refers to Himself as "I am"—Yahweh, God's Old Testament name—and thereby prompts the Pharisees actually to pick up rocks to stone Him for blasphemy. In John 20:28, Jesus tells "Doubting Thomas" to touch His nail-scarred hands and feet. Thomas, in a moment of pure worship, declares "My Lord and my God."

Second, Jesus is not only called God in the Bible, He is also credited with the activity of God (for example, creation in Colossians 1, and John 1). In this regard, it may be helpful to take a notebook and begin writing down everything that the New Testament says about Jesus (clearly, you will fill more than one notebook). The thousands of references point to one conclusion: Jesus is God.

▶ *Was/is Jesus human?* We will address this question in the next session. Christians have long believed that Jesus was fully God and fully human.

▶ *Is Jesus eternal?* Philippians 2 talks about Jesus setting aside His divinity so that He could be born as a human, and passages like Colossians 1 and John 1 place Jesus in the position of co-creator of the universe with the Father. His entrance into the human world was not the beginning, but a continuation, of His life and work. As Jesus said in John 8:58, "before Abraham was, I am!" That statement refers to His eternal power and existence.

▼ ▼ ▼ ▼ ▼ ▼ ▼ ▼ ▼ ▼ ▼ ▼ ▼ ▼ ▼ ▼ ▼ ▼
Additional Resources

1. Kennedy, D. James and Jerry Newcombe. *What If Jesus Had Never Been Born?* Nashville, Tenn.: Thomas Nelson, 1994.

2. Witherington, Ben. *The Jesus Quest: The Third Search for the Jew of Nazareth.* Downers Grove, Ill.: InterVarsity, 1995.

3. Yancey, Philip. *The Jesus I Never Knew.* Grand Rapids, Mich.: Zondervan, 1995.

We Believe in Jesus Christ: Born, Suffered, Crucified

▼ ▼ ▼ ▼ ▼ ▼ ▼ ▼ ▼ ▼ ▼ ▼ ▼ ▼ ▼ ▼ ▼ ▼ ▼ ▼
Overview   10 minutes

❶ *Allow several people to share what they learned from their homework (if the group did not do homework, ask several people to recap what they learned from the last session). Then ask someone to read aloud this overview and the objectives that follow.*

In recent years magazines, newspapers, and television programs have documented a "search for the historical Jesus." Scholars have attempted to reconstruct Jesus' life using sources other than Scripture, and according to their own hypotheses.

The results have been interesting, to say the least. Some say Jesus was a political liberationist. Others claim He was a Greek sage. Then there are those who cast Him as a wicked priest who eloped with Mary Magdalene, a shaman-like guru, a Jewish cynic, and a magician.[1]

We might conclude from this "search" that it's impossible to agree on who Jesus was. Or, we can turn to the simply stated teachings of Scripture—and the records of countless thousands who have lived and died for Him—to learn about Him. In this session we will:

- ▶ discuss our ability to trust people
- ▶ examine what Scripture says about Jesus' humanity and purpose
- ▶ discuss how we are saved through Jesus
- ▶ offer our testimonies of how we met Jesus

41

Beginning
15 minutes

❶ *Go around the room and allow each person to answer the first question before moving on to the next one. The leader should answer first each time.*

1. Who is someone (other than God) you have trusted? What made that person trustworthy?

2. When it comes to trust, which is most true of you?
   - ❏ I trust willingly and freely.
   - ❏ I trust when someone proves trustworthy.
   - ❏ I am slow and reluctant to trust.
   - ❏ I do not trust anyone.

3. Why do you think it is difficult for many people to put complete trust in others?

The Text
5 minutes

John was one of Jesus' original twelve disciples. He traveled an adventurous road with Jesus, witnessing His crucifixion and resurrection. In John 1, John wrote about Jesus' identity, His entrance into the world, and His purpose for arriving.

❶ *Have someone read the text aloud. You may also read some or all of the reference notes on page 47.*

The **Word** was first,
    the Word present to God,
    God present to the Word.
The Word was God,
    in readiness for God from day one.

Everything was created through him;
    nothing—not one thing!—
    came into being without him.
What came into existence was **Life**,
    and the Life was **Light** to live by.
The Life-Light blazed out of the darkness;
    the darkness couldn't put it out. . . .

The Life-Light was the real thing:
    Every person entering Life
    he brings into Light.
He was in the world,
    the world was there through him,
    and yet the world didn't even notice.
He came to his own people,
    but they didn't want him.
But whoever did want him,
    who believed he was who he claimed
    and would do what he said,
He made to be **their true selves**,
    their child-of-God selves.
These are the **God-begotten,**
    not blood-begotten,
    not flesh-begotten,
    not sex-begotten.

The Word became flesh and blood,
    and moved into the neighborhood.
We saw the glory with our own eyes,
    the one-of-a-kind glory,
    like Father, like Son,
Generous inside and out,
    true from start to finish.

(John 1:1-5,10-14, MSG)

4. There are several provocative images used for Christ in this passage, including:

    a. The Word. How does God speak through Jesus?

    b. The Life. How does God offer life through Jesus?

    c. The Light. How does Jesus bring light to the world?

The Incarnation (the embodiment of God in human form) is foundational to Christian thought. Through the incarnation of Jesus we can learn about God's love (look what He does for us), God's power (even His weakness is stronger than sin, death, and evil), God's purpose (He doesn't sit outside of creation and pull strings; He shows us His love in tangible ways), God's tools (He doesn't coerce; He provides an opportunity for our choice), and God's intent (to create a kingdom that is "out of this world," transcending culture and gender).

5. What was the world's response to Jesus?

6. How did "His own people" respond to Him?

7. Why do you suppose both groups responded as they did?

Applying the Text   20 minutes

8. In light of this passage, discuss the importance of these statements from the Apostles' Creed. What does each of them reveal about who Jesus is and what He does?

    ❒ He was born of the Virgin Mary—not begotten by blood, flesh, or sex.
    ❒ He suffered under Pontius Pilate—the world He created rejected Him.
    ❒ He was crucified—His own people didn't want Him.
    ❒ He died and was buried—the Life allowed Himself to be killed.

9. When you think about the conflict and pain evident in these parts of the creed, what thoughts and feelings go through your mind?

10. Based on our text, how would you respond to the following persons?

    a. Gail thinks Jesus was simply a good man, a wise teacher. He was not God.

    b. Diane believes there are many ways to be saved. Jesus is just one of them.

❶ *Allow anyone who wishes to answer questions 11-13. Unless you have no time limitations, try to limit each answer to three minutes.*

11. According to John 1, our response to Jesus is to believe in His name. At what point in your life did you recognize your need for Jesus?

45

12. When and how did you come to believe in Him?

13. What has your life been like since becoming a follower of Jesus?

Assignment   5 minutes

During the upcoming week, locate at least one television show, movie, book, or other form of popular media that demonstrates humanity's desire to be saved (for example, a "good-versus-evil" cartoon).

Prayer   5 minutes

If some in the group have never taken the opportunity to invite Jesus into their lives, now might be the time! If you like, you may say a simple prayer to ask Jesus to be your Savior and Lord. A sample prayer: "Lord, I have studied about you these past few weeks and have come to believe that you are the answer for my life. Please forgive my sins and be my Master forever. Amen."

Others in the group may have been following Jesus for some time. This could be an opportunity to thank Him for the relationship you have had with Him.

Stand in a circle. Hold hands if you are comfortable doing so. Go around the circle, allowing each person who feels comfortable to pray. If you prefer to pray silently, please say, "Amen" aloud so that others will know you are finished.

Reference Notes

Setting: John wrote this gospel so that "you may believe that Jesus is the Christ, the Son of God, and that by believing you may have life in his name" (John 20:31).

Word . . . Life . . . Light: Three graphic images of Jesus. As God the spoken Word He reveals God's truth and was co-creator of the universe. As the Light He is the source of everything that is good, nourishing, and life-giving. As the Life He possesses in Himself eternity and salvation, putting Him in a position to save us.

their true selves: Scripture teaches that in our sin-state, we are a twisted image of what we were created by God to be. Only Jesus can restore us to our God-centered wholeness.

God-begotten, not blood-begotten, not flesh-begotten, not sex-begotten: Several key ideas are found in these words. First, John wants it clearly known that salvation is offered only through God. This is not something attained through relations ("my parents go to church"), activity ("I'm a good enough person"), or human will ("I did this myself"). Second, it is no doubt a back-door comment on Jesus' birth: born of a virgin, He was not "blood-begotten, not flesh-begotten, not sex-begotten (but God-begotten)."

Food for Thought

"I believe in Jesus . . . born of the Virgin Mary, suffered under Pontius Pilate, was crucified, died, and was buried. He descended to the dead."

▶ *Was Jesus really born of a virgin?* It takes faith to accept the Virgin Birth. To think that God somehow used a simple Jewish virgin to "birth" God is an incredible thought, an astounding feat of genetic engineering, to say the least. But Matthew and Luke both go out of their way to explain in some detail that Jesus was born of a virgin. We can either accept this on faith, or question it. The implications to theology are strong: Our view of the Virgin Birth affects our view of Scripture (is it true, or human-manipulated?), of Jesus (how was He able to retain His divinity in a human body without the Virgin Birth?), of Mary (why was she chosen? was she perfect?), and of miracles (does God really perform miracles, or do we live in a naturalistic world?).

▶ *Why Pontius Pilate?* The Creed mentions Pilate alone of all the people who were involved in Jesus' execution. Why? Because he represents earthly power and authority interacting with the eternal God. In the end, the earthly power loses. Also, the reference to the Roman governor is a way of setting the Crucifixion in history (a modern equivalent might be "during the Reagan presidency"). This is not a mythological story, but a historical event.

▶ *How do we view Jesus' crucifixion?* Scripture uses several images to reveal the purpose and work of Jesus' death. Among them are atonement ("at-one-ment" involves bringing together two estranged people), reconciliation (removal of hatred and enmity, Jesus' bridging of the gap between God and repentant humans who had rebelled against God), justification (to acquit or declare not guilty, which is what God does to us in light of Jesus' work), redemption (our purchase from sin's slavery), and propitiation (to pacify someone's anger, in this case God's anger toward sin). Each of these images offers a somewhat different perspective of Christ and His work. None of the images is complete in itself—it relies on others to tell the whole story of Jesus' death on the cross.

Additional Resources

1. Lewis, C. S. *Mere Christianity.* New York: Macmillan, 1943.

2. Lucado, Max. *Six Hours One Friday; He Still Moves Stones.* Sisters, Oreg.: Multnomah, 1993

---

1. James Edwards, "Who Do Scholars Say That I Am?" *Christianity Today,* March 4, 1996.

We Believe in Jesus Christ: On the Third Day He Rose Again

▼ ▼ ▼ ▼ ▼ ▼ ▼ ▼ ▼ ▼ ▼ ▼ ▼ ▼ ▼ ▼ ▼ ▼ ▼ ▼

Overview   10 minutes

❶ *Allow several people to share what they learned from their homework (if the group did not do homework, ask several people to recap what they learned from the last session). Then ask someone to read aloud this overview and the objectives that follow.*

It's easy to believe in theory that Jesus rose from the dead yet to live our days as though it never happened. We give our lives to Christ and begin walking a new road. With God's help we make several changes and begin to believe we're getting somewhere. Then, when God wants to deal with deep character issues (often through suffering or spiritually dry times), we are shocked. God's power seems well suited for the simple things of life, but not for issues like fear, shame, and hidden sin. These deeper issues we much prefer to keep to ourselves.

We begin to live in a no-man's land somewhere between the power of sin and death, and God's power. Sometimes we let sin, shame, or fear control us. At other times we submit to God's work inside us, and we are set free to live in a joy-filled pattern.

On Good Friday Jesus took all of our sins on the cross, and He died to pay sin's penalty. On Easter Sunday, Jesus rose from the dead, utterly defeating sin and death. And every day that we walk with God, we can tap into that power as sin and death are continuously rolled back. In this session we will:

- ▶ share feelings and thoughts related to our faith and goodness
- ▶ examine scriptural connection between Jesus' resurrection and our growth
- ▶ reflect on the lifestyle and motives of a committed follower of Jesus Christ

Beginning   15 minutes

❶ *Go around the room and allow each person to answer the first question before moving on to the next one. The leader may choose to answer first each time.*

1. What is something you did before age eighteen that made you feel guilty?

2. Have you ever felt a deep level of forgiveness from another person or from God?

3. How would you rate your current level of goodness?

    ❐ 5—near perfect
    ❐ 4—getting there
    ❐ 3—making progress
    ❐ 2—this is an uphill climb
    ❐ 1—don't ask

4. What is an area of your life that you would like God to have greater control over?

    ❐ my thought life
    ❐ a bad habit
    ❐ a fear that grips me
    ❐ my management of time, money, eating, or . . .
    ❐ bitterness that has never left me
    ❐ other:

The Text 5 minutes

Christian growth is not rooted in human goodness or ability to change. It is based instead on the resurrection of Jesus Christ from the dead. Growing Christians do not perceive Jesus' resurrection as a fable, nor do they see it as a one-time event to be celebrated once per year. Instead, they find in Jesus' defeat of sin the victory and motivation necessary to continue growing. First Corinthians 15 is a powerful statement on the Resurrection and its present and future implications. The portion of the passage we will focus on deals with how the Resurrection energizes us to grow in our Christian life.

❶ *Have someone read the text aloud. You may also read some or all of the reference notes on pages 55-56.*

Friends, let me go over the Message with you one final time—this Message that I proclaimed and that you made your own; this Message on which you took your stand and by which your life has been saved. (I'm assuming, now, that your belief was the real thing and not a passing fancy, that you're in this for good and holding fast.)

The first thing I did was place before you what was placed so emphatically before me: that the Messiah died for our sins, **exactly as Scripture tells it**; that he was buried; that he was raised from death on the third day, again exactly as Scripture says; that he presented himself alive to Peter, then to his closest followers, and later to more than five hundred of his followers all at the same time, most of them still around (although a few have since died). . . .

Now, let me ask you something profound yet troubling. If you became believers because you trusted the proclamation that Christ is alive, risen from the dead, how can you let people say that there is no such thing as a resurrection? If there's no resurrection, there's no living Christ. And face it—if there's no resurrection for Christ, everything we've told you is smoke and mirrors, and everything you've staked your life on is smoke and mirrors. Not only that, but we would be guilty of telling a string of barefaced lies about God, all these affidavits we passed on to you verifying that God raised up Christ—**sheer fabrications, if there's no resurrection.**

If corpses can't be raised, then Christ wasn't, because he was indeed dead. And if Christ wasn't raised, then all you're doing is wandering about in the dark, as lost as ever. It's even worse for those who died hoping in Christ and resurrection, because they're already in their graves. If all we get out of Christ is a little inspiration for a few short years, we're a pretty sorry lot. But the truth is that Christ *has* been raised up, the first in a long legacy of those who are going to leave the cemeteries.

(1 Corinthians 15:1-6,12-19, MSG)

Understanding the Text   10 minutes

5. Parts of the second paragraph of this passage read like portions of the Apostles' Creed. Why do you think Paul used phrases like "as Scripture tells it" several times in relation to the events of Christ's death and resurrection?

6. Paul lists several individuals and one group who saw Jesus after He rose from the dead. Among them were Jesus' disciples, who were very different after His ascension into heaven than they were before His death a few weeks earlier. They were more focused, prayerful, humble, and Spirit-empowered. How might seeing the resurrected Christ have empowered their faith?

In the third and fourth paragraphs, Paul observes that without the Resurrection there is no living Christ, and we are wandering in the dark.

7. Why is a living Christ so vital to Christian faith and growth?

8. Why does losing a living Christ create darkness and lostness?

9. The foundation for our walk with Christ is that "Christ has been raised up, the first in a long legacy of those who are going to leave the cemeteries." How does Jesus' defeat of sin and death provide power to His followers?

Applying the Text   20 minutes

10. What words would you use to describe a person who walks with Christ, experiencing His power and illumination?

The Resurrection affects believers in several ways: First, it reminds us that God's power is greater than the darkest sin or most painful death. Second, it declares that both sin and death have been utterly defeated, and that we who had nothing to do with their defeat are to celebrate the victory. Third, it challenges us to leave our sins with Jesus on Good Friday and to celebrate instead His victory—thus renewing our focus and taking us away from self-absorbed defeatism.

11. For each of these persons, discuss which of these benefits of the Resurrection applies.

   ❐ Mary worries constantly that she does not measure up to God's standards.
   ❐ John doesn't deal with his sins.
   ❐ Sandy tries hard to be good.
   ❐ Jill embraces God each day and lives in repentant joy.
   ❐ Alan rationalizes his sin by blaming his past.

12. How should Jesus' resurrection impact our spiritual growth?

In order for believers to experience Jesus' resurrection power, we must embrace our part in the spiritual growth process. Our part consists of daily habits, or disciplines, like:

► reflecting on our experiences, reactions, and feelings
► confessing our sins to God and others
► praying for God to empower us and cause us to grow
► meditating slowly and carefully on portions of Scripture

13. For each of these disciplines:

❏ Discuss why Christians might not like doing it.
❏ Explore how its absence might hurt a Christian's growth.
❏ Discuss how it helps us accept God's power in our lives.

▼ ▼

Assignment   5 minutes

Encourage one another to carry a note pad around this week. As you experience feelings, challenges to your faith, or temptations, make notes to yourself. See if you can learn one thing about how you interact in your world:

► Is there a time of day when my struggles are greatest?

► Are there people I have an especially difficult time being around? Why?

► Are there attitudes, actions, and fears that have driven my behavior for my whole life? If so, what are they, where do they come from, and how can I pray for release?

▼ ▼
Prayer   20 minutes

In several moments of quiet, reflect on your past day or so.

> ▶ When did you not respond in a Christlike manner?
> ▶ What does this incident tell you about your strengths
> and weaknesses?

Have someone read Psalm 32 slowly. While the person reads,
listen for what happens to the person who is honest before God.
Afterward, discuss what you heard.

As you feel the freedom, some of you may share what you
reflected on in the quiet, confessing your sins in an atmosphere
of acceptance and love.

Pray for each other, asking God to energize each person's
faith. Do not judge each other or pray for God to fix each other.
Instead, ask for Jesus' resurrection power to be made manifest
in each life.

▼ ▼
Reference Notes

Setting: Paul wrote 1 Corinthians to a gifted yet fractious group
of Christians living in the city of Corinth. Their faith was sometimes powerful but inconsistent.

exactly as Scripture tells it: This statement strongly implies
that some in the church (or those on the fringe) were question-
ing the authority of Scripture and the reality of the resurrection
of Jesus from the dead. Paul makes no concessions, standing
firmly on Scripture and the historic reality of Jesus' resurrection
from the dead.

sheer fabrications, if there's no resurrection: Some apolo-
gists (including Josh McDowell and Charles Colson) have
observed that, with as many followers as Jesus had, it is impossible that they could have created and followed through on a
hoax involving Christ's resurrection. Most people will fabricate

reality in order to get ahead in life. But in the case of Jesus' disciples, as many as 11 of the 12 died for their beliefs. If there was no resurrection, what was the point?

Food for Thought ▼▼▼▼▼▼▼▼▼▼▼▼▼▼▼▼▼▼

"I believe in Jesus. . . . On the third day He rose again. He ascended into heaven, and is seated at the right hand of the Father. He will come again to judge the living and the dead."

▶ *Did Jesus rise from the dead?* Various theories include that He "swooned" and that the disciples came and stole His body. These theories require more faith than does simple belief in His resurrection. The fact is that there were too many people around for the disciples to have perpetrated a hoax, and the Roman soldiers were responsible for making sure Christ was dead before they were allowed to take Him off the cross. Like other facets of Christian belief, faith is required.

▶ *What does He do on the right hand of God?* In Hebrew thought, the right hand represents honor and power. According to Colossians 3, Jesus sits at God's right hand, acting as our high priest: praying for us, working in our lives, ruling with God, building His church, and preparing for His return.

Additional Resources ▲▼▼▼▼▼▼▼▼▼▼▼▼▼▼▼▼▼

1. Bridges, Jerry. *The Pursuit of Holiness*. Colorado Springs, Colo.: NavPress, 1978.

2. Bridges, Jerry. *The Practice of Godliness*. Colorado Springs, Colo.: NavPress, 1983.

3. McDowell, Josh. *More Than a Carpenter*. Wheaton, Ill.: Tyndale, 1985.

We Believe in the Holy Spirit

Overview   10 minutes

❶ *Allow several people to share what they learned from their homework (if the group did not do homework, ask several people to recap what they learned from the last session). Then ask someone to read aloud this overview and the objectives that follow.*

"The wind blows wherever it pleases. You hear its sound, but you cannot tell where it comes from or where it is going. So it is with everyone born of the Spirit" (John 3:8).

One day, as I was driving down the highway, I began to mentally rehearse an argument I was going to have with one of my friends. In the midst of this imaginary dialogue (which, incidentally, I was winning quite handily!), I casually directed a thought to God. *Father, can you believe how hard it is to love this person?*

I was not prepared for God's response—and He *did* respond. Strongly over-ruling my other thoughts, He made His point. *Yes, I can believe how difficult that person is to love. You see, I love you as well!*

By the grace of God, I was given a glimpse of my own difficult side. My stubbornness, pride, and sin were exposed, and I began to see myself as one more rebellious child, deeply loved by the Father.

At first with remorse, and then with laughter, I recognized the irony of my situation. Overlooking the log in my own eye, here I was noticing a small sliver in my friend's eye.

In that moment I felt touched by God. My heart opened to Him, and He filled me with a peace I had rarely known before.

My moment of grace was a gift from the Spirit of God. He communicated with me. He convicted me. He forgave me. He filled me. He does all of this, and more. Likened in Scripture to a legal counselor, a wind, a comforter, a mark of God's intention to save us, a giver of gifts, a creator of "fruit" in our lives, and much more, the Holy Spirit's presence in our lives is what changes us and draws us to the God of the universe.

In this session we will:

- ▶ share our own experiences of the Spirit
- ▶ examine what the Bible says about the Spirit
- ▶ discuss a healthy approach to things of the Spirit

▼ ▼ ▼ ▼ ▼ ▼ ▼ ▼ ▼ ▼ ▼ ▼ ▼ ▼ ▼ ▼ ▼ ▼ ▼
Beginning   15 minutes

❶ *Go around the room and allow each person to answer the first question. The leader may choose to answer first.*

1. What picture comes to mind when you hear the words, "Holy Spirit"?

2. The following are some ways in which people experience the Holy Spirit. Tell about a time when you have experienced one of these.

   ❐ an intense awareness of God's presence
   ❐ an unusual healing
   ❐ joy in a difficult situation
   ❐ insight into how a passage of the Bible applied to me
   ❐ finally realizing that Jesus is the Son of God
   ❐ guidance as to what to say or do in a situation

- [ ] the ability to resist a temptation
- [ ] freedom from a compulsive habit
- [ ] I'm new at all this, and I'm not sure I've experienced the Holy Spirit.
- [ ] other:

The Text   5 minutes

Paul was angry when he wrote Galatians, a letter in which he reminds believers in Galatia that they are not to fall back into legalistic Judaism but are instead to focus on God's grace through Jesus Christ. In chapter 5 he contrasts a self-centered religious lifestyle with a Spirit-filled lifestyle.

❶ *Have someone read the text aloud. You may also read some or all of the reference notes on pages 62-63.*

My counsel is this: Live freely, animated and motivated by God's Spirit. Then you won't feed the compulsions of **selfishness**. For there is a root of sinful self-interest in us that is at odds with a free spirit, just as the free spirit is incompatible with selfishness. These two ways of life are antithetical, so that you cannot live at times one way and at times another way according to how you feel on any given day. Why don't you choose to be led by the Spirit and so escape the erratic compulsions of a law-dominated existence?

It is obvious what kind of life develops out of trying to get your own way all the time: repetitive, loveless, cheap sex; a stinking accumulation of mental and emotional garbage; frenzied and joyless grabs for happiness; trinket gods; magic-show religion; paranoid loneliness; cutthroat competition; all-consuming-yet-never-satisfied wants; a brutal temper; an impotence to love or be loved; divided homes and divided lives; small-minded and lopsided pursuits; the vicious habit of depersonalizing everyone into a rival; uncontrolled and uncontrollable addictions; ugly parodies of community. I could go on.

This isn't the first time I have warned you, you know. If you use your freedom this way, **you will not inherit God's kingdom**.

But what happens when we live God's way? He brings gifts into our lives, much the same way that fruit appears in an orchard—things like affection for others, exuberance about life, serenity. We develop a willingness to stick with things, a sense of compassion in the heart, and a conviction that a basic holiness permeates things and people. We find ourselves involved in loyal commitments, not needing to force our way in life, able to marshal and direct our energies wisely.

Legalism is helpless in bringing this about; it only gets in the way. Among those who belong to Christ, everything connected with getting our own way and mindlessly responding to what everyone else calls necessities is killed off for good—crucified.

Since this is the kind of life we have chosen, the life of the Spirit, let us make sure that we do not just hold it as an idea in our heads or a sentiment in our hearts, but work out its implications in every detail of our lives. That means we will not compare ourselves with each other as if one of us were better and another worse. We have far more interesting things to do with our lives. Each of us is an original.

(Galatians 5:16-26, MSG)

Understanding the Text   10 minutes

3. According to this passage, what does the Holy Spirit do?

4. How does the Spirit change us into new people?

5. How do we participate with the Spirit in this process?

6. If a Christian isn't experiencing a consistent increase in the kind of "fruit" Paul describes, what counsel would you give?

7. According to this text, to be led by the Spirit is to "live freely, animated and motivated by God's Spirit." What would be a practical example of someone doing that?

Applying the Text   20 minutes

8. A Spirit-led lifestyle produces changes (fruit). Paul lists them in the fourth paragraph of our text, beginning with "things like affection for others." Choose one fruit and tell why you need the Spirit to produce this in you.

9. The Spirit is present in the lives of believers, setting us free from the past and producing God's character in us. Based on this passage (and taking into account other things you might know about the Holy Spirit), try to describe to each other:

   ❏ who the Spirit is
   ❏ what the Spirit's role in our salvation and growth is
   ❏ how our lives are impacted when the Spirit is in control

A three-legged stool can illustrate the three functions the Spirit wants to have in our lives. The first leg is *truth*—the Spirit wants to teach us about Christ and how to follow Him. The second leg is *experience*—the Spirit draws us into a relationship with God, then grants us power and gifts for use in His service. The third leg is *fruit*—the Spirit softens us and brings God's character into our lives.

10. Which "leg" is strongest in your life? For example, you might have a lot of knowledge about God (truth).

11. Which "leg" do you feel needs God's work in your life?

Assignment   5 minutes

Partner with God in prayer, addressing one of your revealed weaknesses (truth, experience, or fruit).

► If *truth* was your weakness, you may want to read and reflect on texts like Romans 8, John 14, and John 16. Make a list of everything said about the Spirit.

► If *experience* is your weakness, ask God to touch your life in one special way this coming week. Then pay close attention to your experiences, to see how God touches you.

► If *fruit* is your weakness, meditate on Galatians 5:22-23. Think about what each fruit involves. Pray for God to build the missing fruit into your life.

Prayer   5 minutes

Stand in a circle. Beginning with the leader, complete this statement for the person on your right: "One thing I have learned about you from being in this group is. . . ." Let each person pray aloud, beginning with the leader. Thank God for what you are learning, and pray together that God's work will continue and expand. If you would rather pray silently, please say "Amen" aloud to let the other people know you are finished.

Reference Notes

Setting: Paul wrote Galatians to churches he had founded in Asia Minor (modern Turkey).

selfishness: A good translation of the Greek word for "flesh." Our flesh is at its root self-occupied.

you will not inherit God's kingdom: Not only is legalistic living shallow and self-centered, but it is antithetical to the Spirit's work in our lives. It is evidence that He is not there.

Food for Thought

"I believe in the Holy Spirit."

▶ *What is the Spirit's role in our conversion?* The waters of baptism are the symbol of the Spirit's cleansing. They point to our belief that when we commit ourselves to Christ, the Spirit enters us and washes our sins away.

▶ *When are we baptized in the Spirit?* Many traditions believe that baptism in the Spirit occurs when a person invites Jesus Christ into his or her life. These traditions affirm that we need to be "filled with the Spirit" many times in our lives, but we are baptized in the Spirit only once. Others believe that all Christians should seek a second baptism (like the experience of the disciples in Acts 2). These traditions note that the disciples were already committed followers of Jesus Christ, yet Jesus told them in Acts 1:5 that they were about to be baptized in the Spirit. Both traditions agree that a maturing Christian will be continually yielding himself or herself to the Spirit's inner work and outer manifestation.

▶ *Are spiritual gifts still viable in the church?* Yes. Several passages in Scripture contain lists of spiritual gifts, including 1 Corinthians 12 and Romans 12. These passages say that God gives all believers some gift which they are to apply in God's church. The point of controversy is not whether the Spirit gifts people; it is which gifts are still viable. Some believe, for example, that miraculous gifts ceased after the deaths of the apostles (citing 1 Corinthians 13:8-10) or the closing of the canon of Scripture. Others believe that all gifts (including those associated with the offices of apostle and prophet) are to be used in Christ's church.

► *What about some people who claim to have been so touched by the Spirit that they faint or experience other physical manifestations like tongues and healing?* Such experiences have been documented throughout church history, most notably in the Great Awakenings of the 1700s and later. Believers have often experienced God in strange and unique ways. How are we to understand these manifestations? First, we admit that although God is changeless and eternal, He relates to each of us in a different manner. Second, we acknowledge that we often perceive our experiences in an incomplete manner. Scripture says that God works everything to the good of those who love Him. Often He does His greatest work through our defeats, stresses, and suffering. Any person who describes his or her experience needs to be careful to speak in the "I", not the "you" (as in, "you need what I've got!"). Third, we understand that the result of a genuine touch from God is the softening of our heart, making us more like Christ. We don't need to prove our experiences to others; we just need to walk with God, letting the fruit speak for the results.

▼▼▼▼▼▼▼▼▼▼▼▼▼▼▼▼▼▼▼
Additional Resources

1. Fee, Gordon. *God's Empowering Presence*. Peabody, Mass.: Hendrickson, 1994.

2. Fee, Gordon. *Paul, the Spirit, and the People of God*. Peabody, Mass.: Hendrickson, 1996. (This volume is a concentrated version of *God's Empowering Presence*. It presents in 200 pages what is thoroughly developed and documented in that 700 page volume.)

3. Stott, John R. W. *Baptism and Fullness*. Downers Grove, Ill.: InterVarsity, 1976

We Believe in the Holy Christian Church

Overview ▼▼▼▼▼▼▼▼▼▼▼▼▼▼▼▼▼ 10 minutes

❶ *Allow several people to share what they learned from their homework (if the group did not do homework, ask several people to recap what they learned from the last session). Then ask someone to read aloud this overview and the objectives that follow.*

"Isn't the bride beautiful today?"

These words are often said at weddings. Women may go to great extremes to adorn themselves so that their walk down the aisle makes their partner beam. From hair to nails to makeup to dress and more, the details are attended to with great care.

"Isn't the bride beautiful today?"

These are also the words of Scripture. The church is likened to the bride of Christ in Ephesians 5 and Revelation 21. In Revelation, the bride (the "new Jerusalem") is presented in unfathomable splendor as she prepares for a new day in partnership with Jesus. In Ephesians we discover the source of the church's beauty: Christ's sacrificial love causes the church to be presented to Him as clean and pure.

Unfortunately, it's difficult to imagine such purity and beauty from where we stand. Characteristics that we call ugly are part of even the best churches: back-biting, self-interest, self-deceit, stubbornness, and a host of other maladies.

Many turn away from the church. "I can worship just as well at home by myself, or walking through the woods," they suggest. But then, if we are God's people, don't we need to get along with God's bride?

"Isn't the bride beautiful today?"

Sometimes when I am standing in the back of our sanctuary on a Sunday morning, my wife will sidle up to me as I survey the unique collection of persons preparing for worship. She will whisper those words, and I will smile.

The bride is often not beautiful, but I am finding as I mature that my attraction to her is in direct proportion to my desire to sacrifice for her. Christ loves the church, and sees something beautiful in her. He calls us to love her as well.

In this session we will:

▶ discuss some of our experiences with the church
▶ examine what Scripture says about the church's identity, purpose, and power
▶ reflect on our role in making the church stronger

▼ ▼ ▼ ▼ ▼ ▼ ▼ ▼ ▼ ▼ ▼ ▼ ▼ ▼ ▼ ▼ ▼ ▼ ▼
Beginning   15 minutes

❶ *Go around the room and allow each person to answer the first question before moving to the next one.*

1. What is your ethnic heritage (countries, specific peoples)?

2. Choose one of the following categories and tell a brief story about your ancestors or immediate family:

   ❏ an interesting personality
   ❏ an unusual event
   ❏ a historic or famous incident
   ❏ a unique relationship

3. What is one way, either positive or negative, that your life has been affected by your attachment to your extended or ancestral family?

4. Christians are part of God's family. Just as our family stories are woven into our personal stories, so our church
experience is woven into our faith stories. Choose one of
the following and share a fun "church" story you experienced at some point in your life.

❐ a person from church who reflected God in a curious
way
❐ an event that was unusual
❐ an incident that was important to you
❐ a relationship (involving you) that was strained

▼ ▼ ▼ ▼ ▼ ▼ ▼ ▼ ▼ ▼ ▼ ▼ ▼ ▼ ▼ ▼ ▼ ▼ ▼

The Text   5 minutes

First Peter 2 provides perhaps the clearest expression in
Scripture of the identity, purpose, and power of the church. Far
from being merely lofty rhetoric, it builds a foundation and
shoots for the stars.

❶ *Have someone read the text aloud. You may also read
some or all of the reference notes on page 71.*

Welcome to the living Stone, the source of life. The workmen
took one look and threw it out; God set it in the place of honor.
Present yourselves as building stones for the construction of a
sanctuary vibrant with life, in which you'll serve as holy **priests**
offering Christ-approved lives up to God. The Scriptures provide
precedent:

"Look! I'm setting a stone in **Zion**,
a cornerstone in the place of honor.
Whoever trusts in this stone as a foundation
will never have cause to regret it."

To you who trust him, he's a Stone to be proud of, but to those
who refuse to trust him,

"The stone the workmen **threw out**
is now the chief foundation stone."

For the untrusting it's

"... a stone to trip over,
a boulder blocking the way."

They trip and fall because they refuse to obey, just as predicted.
But you are the ones chosen by God, chosen for the high calling of priestly work, chosen to be a holy people, God's instruments to do his work and speak out for him, to tell others of the night-and-day difference he made for you—from nothing to something, from rejected to accepted.

(1 Peter 2:4-10, MSG)

▼▼▼▼▼▼▼▼ ▼ ▼ ▼ ▼ ▼ ▼ ▼ ▼ ▼ ▼
Understanding the Text   10 minutes

5. Discuss what each of the following tells us about Jesus.

    ❏ He is the source of life.
    ❏ He was rejected by the workmen, honored by God.
    ❏ He is the cornerstone of Zion (see note, page 71).
    ❏ He is a stumbling stone for the untrusting.

6. Peter speaks of a church built with "living stones."

    a. How different is Peter's "living sanctuary" image from the usual images we think of when we say the word "church"?

    b. What might be characteristics and qualities of a living sanctuary?

7. A significant theme in this passage involves the identity of those who participate with Christ in worshiping God.

    a. What is the role of a priest?

68

b. What does it mean that we are priests?

c. We tend to expect priests to be different (holy and good). What kinds of things will change for the "average Christian" when we place upon ourselves the expectations of priesthood?

8. As God's priests, we are God's instruments to do His work and speak out for Him. What are examples of things we might do and say in that role?

Applying the Text   20 minutes

9. Discuss what this passage teaches us about:
   ❏ how people get involved in Christ's church
   ❏ the church's purposes
   ❏ what makes the church special

10. Discuss what advice, help, or encouragement would you give in the following situations based on what you have learned from this passage?

    ❏ A small, rural church is slowly dying and giving up hope.
    ❏ A friend professes faith in Christ but doesn't go to church.
    ❏ A volunteer is frustrated because nobody is helping her.
    ❏ A Christian friend is going through a painful time and does not feel support from God's people.

11. If we are the priests of God's church, then we are to do everything we can to make the church stronger. What is one thing you can do to support your church?

Assignment   5 minutes

Reflect on the implications of your importance to Christ's church by (choose one):

► Interviewing three members of your congregation, asking them what they perceive your church's strengths and weaknesses to be. How might you help to reverse a weakness?

► Interviewing three nonattenders of church, asking them what they perceive the church's strengths and weaknesses to be. How might you help to reverse a weakness?

► Reading through your congregation's annual report, asking the question "How is this a living, breathing congregation filled with Christ's priests?"

   Share the results of your inquiries with the group at your next meeting.

Prayer   5 minutes

Stand in a circle. Hold hands if you are comfortable doing so. Let each person pray aloud, beginning with the leader. Thank God for what you are learning, and pray together for your church and each person's ministry to the church. If you would rather pray silently, please say "Amen" aloud to let the other people know you are finished.

Reference Notes

Setting: Peter wrote this letter to young believers scattered throughout the Roman world. They were undergoing hardship and persecution. Peter's response is to be positive, to employ strong imagery as motivation, and to use many emphatic verbs as an empowering technique, calling "victims" to action.

priests: Does a passage like this negate the ordained ministry? No. God gives spiritual gifts to all His people, some of which are related to preaching, teaching, and pastoring. The apostle Paul wrote several books of the Bible (1 and 2 Timothy and Titus—the "pastoral letters") specifically to church leaders. However, the point of this passage is that each believer now has access to God, a privilege formerly reserved only for priests.

Zion: Another name for Jerusalem. In the New Testament it is used to refer to the new Jerusalem or heaven.

threw out: A visual image hearkening to the days when the work-men constructed the Temple in Jerusalem (which is on a hill), and threw defective stones to the bottom of the hill.

Food for Thought

"I believe in . . . the holy Christian church."

▶ *How do we understand the word "catholic" (versus "Christian") in the older translations of the Apostles' Creed?* The word has a small "c" and is an old English word meaning "universal." It denotes that the church is God's church and is one body. While some denominations and religions may claim universality ("we're the only true church"), we believe that only God can make such a claim. So we do believe in the holy, "catholic" (united) church, understanding that it is God's claim to the church, not ours, that counts.

► *What is the "communion of saints"?* Communion is our participation in salvation (and the Lord's Supper) as a community relationship. In some traditions, saints are heroes who have been awarded titles. But in this context, *saint* refers both to present Christians (who are called saints at various points in Scripture) and to past Christians (who have gone before us into heaven). Our communion is both with the living on earth and with those living in heaven. This image invokes images of the feast we will celebrate together in heaven for eternity. It also reminds us that our local congregation is connected to all the other gatherings of believers around the world.

► *Why does "the forgiveness of sins" occur here in the Apostles' Creed, and not in relation to the work of either Jesus or the Spirit?* In Luke 24:47, Jesus commissioned His disciples to proclaim "repentance and forgiveness of sins" to all nations. This is the work of God's people—to speak about repentance and to minister to one another the forgiveness of Christ. We say in the Lord's Prayer that we expect God to forgive our sins (through Jesus and the Spirit). We also know that we will have to forgive each other as we express God's love to each other.

▼ ▼ ▼ ▼ ▼ ▼ ▼ ▼ ▼ ▼ ▼ ▼ ▼ ▼ ▼ ▼ ▼ ▼ ▼

Additional Resources

1. Colson, Charles. *The Body.* Dallas, Tex.: Word, 1992.

2. Hybels, Bill and Lynne. *The Church You've Always Longed For.* Grand Rapids, Mich.: Zondervan, 1995.

3. Mead, Loren. *The Once and Future Church.* Nashville, Tenn.: Abingdon, 1994.

We Believe in the Life Everlasting

▼ ▼ ▼ ▼ ▼ ▼ ▼ ▼ ▼ ▼ ▼ ▼ ▼ ▼ ▼ ▼ ▼ ▼
Overview
10 minutes

❶ *Allow several people to share what they learned from their homework (if the group did not do homework, ask several people to recap what they learned from the last session). Then ask someone to read aloud this story and the objectives that follow.*

I remember a time when anticipation kept me going. I had been talked into a mission trip to Haiti, somewhat against my will. A college junior, I had just left a youth ministry position I had occupied for two years. I was grieving. The last thing I wanted was to help anybody.

As our plane landed in Haiti and I got my first glimpse of the airport (and waves of heat), I remember touching my seat and inviting the memory of air conditioning and good food to hold me for the next three weeks.

I thought of that air conditioned plane seat often during those three weeks, as I lay awake at night listening to the mosquitoes preparing to attack my face. And of the airplane food that would seem a welcome change from some of what we ate. The anticipation of a way out actually helped me, and I began to relax. That enabled the trip to change me, and I fell in love with Haiti. I have returned several times.

My story is a parable of hope. Biblical hope is the assurance that God has taken care of our future and our eternity. It causes us to look forward with eagerness, even if today is difficult.

Hope is what allows us to face pain, process grief, and overcome sin. Without hope a Christian is doomed—for when the way becomes difficult, we will want to quit. With hope a Christian is saved—for instead of obsessing about current and past struggles, we fix our eyes on a point far into the distance and keep walking.

Discussing eternity as the basis of hope is important for Christians. In this session we will:

▶ process what this group experience has taught us
▶ share some of the things that motivate us in life
▶ discuss what Scripture says about Christ's return
▶ consider ways that Christ's return can give us an identity and sense of hope

▼ ▼ ▼ ▼ ▼ ▼ ▼ ▼ ▼ ▼ ▼ ▼ ▼ ▼ ▼ ▼ ▼ ▼ ▼
Beginning   15 minutes

❶ *Choose either question 1 or 2. (You may do both if you have time.) Then cover both questions 3 and 4. Go around the room and allow each person to answer the first question before moving on to the next one.*

1. Finish this sentence for someone in the group: One thing I have learned from you because of our involvement in this group is. . . .

2. Finish this sentence: One thing I have appreciated about this group experience is. . . .

3. Choose one of the following that best describes you:

   ❏ I eagerly get out of bed, ready to face the day.
   ❏ I am a slow starter in the morning, but optimistic about most days.
   ❏ I am a slow starter in the morning, and pessimistic about most days.
   ❏ I hate getting of bed and facing the day.

4. Everybody has something or someone that "keeps them going" (gives them hope). Which one of the following is an example of something that helps you to focus on living, even during difficult times?

☐ family—they support and sustain me
☐ friends—I don't know where I'd be without them
☐ fear—if I don't keep going, it's all going to catch up with me
☐ faith—I have no control over anything, but rest assured in God's promises
☐ fact—this is what I've got to get done today
☐ fantasy—maybe tomorrow will be better than today

5. Which of the above is closest to biblical hope (which roots itself in the trustworthiness of God)?

▼ ▼ ▼ ▼ ▼ ▼ ▼ ▼ ▼ ▼ ▼ ▼ ▼ ▼ ▼ ▼ ▼ ▼ ▼ ▼
The Text
5 minutes

Eternity and the end of time are significant topics in Scripture. From the words of Jesus, to significant portions in several New Testament letters, to the book of Revelation, we can trace end time themes through Scripture. In this session's passage, Paul considers the essential elements of the second coming of Christ.

❶ *Have someone read the text aloud. You may also read some or all of the reference notes on page 79.*

This image of planting a dead seed and raising a live plant is a mere sketch at best, but perhaps it will help in approaching the mystery of the resurrection body—but only if you keep in mind that when we're raised, we're raised for *good*, alive forever! The corpse that's planted is no beauty, but when it's raised, it's glorious. Put in the ground weak, it comes up powerful. The seed sown is natural; the seed grown is supernatural—same seed, same body, but what a difference from when it goes down in physical mortality to when it is raised up in spiritual immortality! . . .

I need to emphasize, friends, that our natural, earthy lives don't in themselves lead us by their very nature into the kingdom of God. Their very "nature" is to die, so how could they "naturally" end up in the Life kingdom?

But let me tell you something wonderful, a mystery I'll probably never fully understand. **We're not all going to die—** *but* we are all going to be changed. You hear a blast to end all blasts from a trumpet, and in the time that you look up and blink your eyes—it's over. On signal from that trumpet from heaven, the dead will be up and out of their graves, beyond the reach of death, never to die again. At the same moment and in the same way, we'll all be changed. In the resurrection scheme of things, this has to happen: everything perishable taken off the shelves and replaced by the imperishable, this mortal replaced by the immortal. Then the saying will come true:

> "Death swallowed by triumphant Life!
> Who got the last word, oh, Death?
> Oh, Death, who's afraid of you now?"

It was sin that made death so frightening and law-code guilt that gave sin its leverage, its destructive power. But now in a single victorious stroke of Life, all three—sin, guilt, death—are gone, the gift of our Master, Jesus Christ. Thank God!

With all this going for us, my dear, dear friends, stand your ground. And don't hold back. **Throw yourselves into the work of the Master, confident** that nothing you do for him is a waste of time or effort.

(1 Corinthians 15:42-44,50-58, MSG)

▼ ▼ ▼ ▼ ▼ ▼ ▼ ▼ ▼ ▼ ▼ ▼ ▼ ▼ ▼ ▼ ▼ ▼
Understanding the Text   10 minutes

6. How does the image of a seed in the ground illustrate the resurrection from the dead?

7. Some people believe that every sincere person will be "okay" in the next life. How does the second paragraph dispute that claim ("I need to emphasize, friends . . .")?

8. According to the third paragraph, what are the events that will accompany Jesus' return?

9. Discuss how Jesus defeated each of these:
   ❑ sin
   ❑ death
   ❑ guilt

10. How does our firm hope in the resurrection from the dead allow us to accomplish Paul's commands to stand our ground, don't hold back, and throw ourselves into the work of the Master?

▼▼▼▼▼▼▼▼▼▼▼▼▼▼▼▼▼▼
Applying the Text   20 minutes

11. Christians tend to approach the end times with a variety of motivations. Discuss how each of these negative motives might be addressed by this text:

   ❑ witness—if we can scare unbelievers badly enough by discussing end times, perhaps we can save them
   ❑ control—we read the Scriptures so that we can develop charts defining when and how everything is going to happen
   ❑ fear—world events seem to point to a time of chaos before Jesus returns
   ❑ abandonment—get me out of here!

12. According to our text, what is the appropriate motivation for believers waiting for Jesus' return?

13. Humans are taught to place their value in things they do, in who they are, or in what they hope to accomplish or receive in the future. Even Christians place their value in such things. Discuss how you would explain hope to the following persons without minimizing their pain?

☐ an elderly man in a nursing home slowly losing his memory, who feels valueless
☐ a simple Christian servant who feels as though her contribution to God is minimal
☐ a teen grieving the death of his parents

▼ ▼
Assignment   5 minutes

Discuss what is next for your group, concentrating on the following options:

▶ Shall we continue? If so, what will be our plan for the next six to eighteen weeks?
▶ Shall we end? If so, shall we plan a party?
▶ Shall we end for now, and pick up in the future? If so, when?

▼ ▼ ▼ ▼ ▼ ▼ ▼ ▼ ▼ ▼ ▼ ▼ ▼ ▼ ▼ ▼ ▼ ▼ ▼ ▼
Prayer   5 minutes

Stand in a circle. You may consider completing this sentence: "Lord, we thank you that in these last eight sessions we have learned. . . ." Close by reciting the Creed together.

▼ ▼ ▼ ▼ ▼ ▼ ▼ ▼ ▼ ▼ ▼ ▼ ▼ ▼ ▼ ▼ ▼ ▼ ▼
Reference Notes

Setting: See the reference notes to session 5. This teaching occurs in the greater context of Paul's discussion of Jesus' resurrection from the dead.

We're not all going to die: When Jesus returns, some will be living on earth and will not have to face death.

Throw yourselves into the work of the Master, confident: There is perhaps no better definition of biblical hope. It is not confidence aimed at giving us a happy life. It is confidence that empowers us to serve God against all odds.

▼ ▼ ▼ ▼ ▼ ▼ ▼ ▼ ▼ ▼ ▼ ▼ ▼ ▼ ▼ ▼ ▼ ▼ ▼
Additional Resources

1. Clouse, Robert. *The Meaning of the Millenium: Four Views.* Downers Grove, Ill.: InterVarsity, 1977.

Turn your group into a community.

Most study guides are designed for individual use. While packed with good material, they don't provide much help in the way of group dynamic.

That's where PILGRIMAGE study guides are different. By incorporating community-building questions and exercises into each session, PILGRIMAGE guides will help your group grow closer relationally as you grow deeper spiritually. THE PILGRIMAGE SERIES includes titles like:

Seven Traits of a Successful Leader
by Jeff Arnold

Whether you're teaching a class or leading a group, there are certain character qualities that can significantly increase your impact. This guide will help you develop the seven essential traits of a successful leader.
(ISBN: 1-57683-019-5; 7 sessions; 96 pages)

Seven Tools for Building Effective Groups
by Jeff Arnold

Just as the most talented carpenter would be handicapped without the right tools, there are key skills every effective group leader must possess. This guide features the seven most important.
(ISBN: 1-57683-020-9; 7 sessions; 96 pages)

Experiencing Community
by Thom Corrigan

Whether you're forming a new group or would like to build a stronger bond of community in your existing group, this seven-week study is the perfect "body-builder."
(ISBN: 8-09109-938-7; 7 sessions; 80 pages)

101 Great Ideas to Create a Caring Group
by Thom Corrigan

Many believe the single highest felt need in our society is the need to belong. To know someone else cares about us. Here are 101 proven ideas for cultivating an atmosphere of care in any small group.
(ISBN: 1-57683-072-1; 80 pages)

These and other NavPress study guides are available at your local Christian bookstore. Or call 1-800-366-7788 to order.

NAVPRESS
BRINGING TRUTH TO LIFE